The rights of Susan Johnson-Hewitt to be identified as the Author of this work have been asserted by her in accordance with the Copyright, Designs and Patents Act 1988.

No part of this publication may be reproduced, stored or transmitted in any form or by any means without the prior permission of the publisher in accordance with the terms of licences issued by the Copyright Licensing Agency.

International Copyright ©   Susan Johnson-Hewitt

ISBN: ISBN: 9781709587276
IMPRINT: INDEPENDENTLY PUBLISHED

SPIRITUAL GUIDANCE FOR THOSE WHO
ARE SEARCHING FOR ANSWERS

WHY
is the question

HERE ARE SOME OF THE QUESTIONS WE ASK

INNER PEACE, LOVE, WISDOM, STRENGTH, FREEDOM

PREFACE

I first got involved in spiritualism when I was 23 years old. I had no knowledge of this subject at this point until a friend invited me to an evening where a medium was giving readings. So I went and my Nan came through. She gave me information about my life at that time and referred to a condition my baby son of 6 months was suffering with. I thought he was teething but she told me he had an ear infection. The next day I was bathing him and when I went to wash his ear he pulled away. I took him to the doctors and it was confirmed he had in fact got an ear infection. This was the start of my journey.

I found the nearest spiritualist church and went one Sunday evening, expecting a message. I did not receive a message that evening or for the next 6 weeks that I attended. What did happen though was my growing awareness of the philosophy that was being taught. It was basically down to common sense. Everything resonated with me. As I continued to attend this church I was very lucky to have been lent many books by the kind people in the church. I was the youngest there so they were encouraged to help me learn more. I could not read enough; it was like giving me a key to unlock the door. Once it was opened I recognised so much of what I was reading. There was of course so much more to learn. We are learning until the day we die and return home.

I can truly say, hand on heart that I draw from this spiritual philosophy that has been channelled from many guides to help me through the most difficult times in my life. The time this will help you the most is when you are down on your knees. This knowledge and awareness will give you the inner strength and understanding as to why things happen. Not to blame a higher energy but to accept personal responsibility which I hope you will understand more about once you have read this book. We have a choice in how we choose to react to people and situations. We are each other's teachers. Earth is not an easy school to learn on but this is why we have chosen to come here. Our soul needs the progression earth can give us.

My continuous journey led me to qualify as a teacher in Spiritual Philosophy in 1997. This has enabled me to help to mentor many people on their pathway, either on a one-to-one basis or by attending my courses, talks or workshops. I also run weekly meditation/circles. My other passion is guiding souls into the light who are earthbound. There are very different reasons why people stay around here and choose not to go into the light. My quest is to find out their reasons and to reassure them and alleviate any fears so they go into the light and go home.

I started out doing spiritual healing in 1987 then moved on to qualify as a foot/face Reflexologist and Shiatsu therapist and have been successfully treating people since 1995. As a therapist, I always treat the person as a whole, linking the emotional, mental and physical aspects of my clients together in order to bring balance into their lives.

I dedicate this book
to my dearest sister
Lin.

CONTENTS

Why do children have to die? 10

Why do some people not communicate through mediums after they have passed? 17

How do we understand Suicide? 21

What are the repercussions from mistakes made in my life? 25

Is there free will if everything is planned? 31

What happens after physical death? 37

What are the different Psychic abilities? 45

What happens to animals when they die? 51

How will I know which partner to choose if I've had more than one? 53

Why does a higher energy allow so much
suffering in the world?   57

Why do some people have harder lives than
others?   63

Why can I not remember past lives?   67

Will I meet all my loved ones in the spirit
world?   71

What is quality of life?   75

What is the difference between Guides,
Spirit Helpers and Guardian Angels?   79

What are the different astral planes?   85

Why Do Children Have to Die?

All souls have to have experiences of childhood, whether here on earth, the Spirit World or other planets. As there are no limitations in the Spirit World, just like paradise, it may be necessary for that particular Soul to experience learning their childhood without any restrictions that are imposed on us on earth. To enable this to happen, there has to be contact with an Earthly Body already incarnated on the earth. This is where the painful experience of miscarriage occurs. The grief and heartache this brings can leave an emptiness that cannot be filled for a while.

I have written a short poem, which I would like to share with you that expressed my feelings after experiencing my first miscarriage:

My Miscarriage

I am carrying a child
I feel so much joy
How many times on that phone have I dialled?
Wondering expectantly if it is a girl or a boy

Then all of a sudden out of the blue
The baby is no more
The teachings I know, and this I turn to
Knowing that it is Natural Law

I'm fine for a time
Knowing in my heart it is to be
But there was a baby in this tummy of mine
And I'm crying from deep inside of me

But then I have tried to miss
Which we have not the power to do
The understanding that would be amiss
The lesson and wisdom I had due

So now I try to let it go
The sadness in my heart
So I may understand and grow
That my baby and I will never be apart
This I know.

Susan Johnson-Hewitt

Before we incarnated on earth, we discussed and planned our lives with our higher guides and angels. We also offered our services in love, to be channels for certain souls to touch us to enable them to grow up in the Spirit World. Our earthly minds may reject this but our Spiritual mind, our higher selves will know of the great service we have given. So if some are still feeling the pain and heartache of such an experience I hope these words will give you some comfort to know you have been used as a channel to help another soul in their development.

When a child is born ill or disabled and has a short life here on earth this is indeed an experience needed for both child and parents. The child may need to undertake this lesson for their growth and the same for the parents. The child may have chosen through unconditional love to give parents this experience, these are indeed evolved souls; to give this learning to others with no thought to themselves but to serve, is indeed proof of unconditional love. I also feel parents who have disabled children are very special people. Although the lessons from this can be compassion, patience, tolerance and unconditional love, I feel you need to be on a certain level, be evolved enough, to be able to experience and undertake this type of learning. I have the highest respect for parents in this situation, the way most adapt, accept and draw inner strength and guidance to help them with their daily life with these beautiful, evolved children. The teachings these children bring are priceless and can give such happiness.

We have no recollection of what we may have done in previous lives. All of us have reacted in a negative way in certain situations. We are all still doing so in this lifetime;

that is why we are here! We do not know if we may have been unsympathetic to a disabled child or to a woman who has had miscarriages or even one who has had an abortion. I feel when this situation arises and an abortion is decided upon, which may be one of the hardest decisions one has to make, it is one of those experiences that can enable one to have compassion for another in similar circumstances. Nothing is black or white in life, so we have these experiences to enable us to have more compassion, empathy and love for one another, rather than being Judgmental or Critical.

Most children who go back to Spirit quickly are generally old souls. Even though here for a short time, valuable lessons can be learnt. Children from the Spirit World can also serve our children on the Earth Plane. Many children who are going through a difficult time will have imaginary friends. This is where Spirit Children can support and help the child who is in need. When parents scoff at these imaginary friends they are creating a shut down process within the child, which is so sad as the child is experiencing a natural response to connecting with Spirit. Most children can see Spirit for the first two years; unfortunately we lose this ability as we become so immersed in our Physical World. No encouragement is given with Spiritual Nourishment, so we lose our ability to see psychically. We then go on through life trying to re-capture or search for the very thing we have lost, connection.

Also remember when you are asleep you see your children. There is no time in Spirit so the children will have no conception of morning or night. It is a bit like a day nursery but a hundred times better. I also relate to the poem "God's Lent Child".

This is one of my favourite poems:

*"I'll lend you a child of mine for a time," It was said.
"For you to love the while they lives and grieve for when they are dead.
It may be 4 or 11 years, or twenty-one or three,
But will you, till I call them back, look after them for me?
They will bring to you so much joy, and should their stay be brief,
You'll have their lovely memories as a comfort in your grief."*

*"I cannot guarantee they will stay; since all will return,
But there are teachings taught on earth I want this child to learn.
I've looked the whole globe over to find teachers that are true
And to help in the tapestry of life you have chosen for you.
Now will you give them all your love, not think the struggle is in vain,
Or loathe me when I come to take them back again?*

Do you understand the words 'Dear Lord, Thy will be done!'
For all the happiness this child shall bring, the risk of heartache we will run.
We will surround them with gentleness, we'll love them every day,
And for the happiness we've known, in our hearts this will always stay.
But should the angels call for him much sooner than we've planned,
We'll brave the piercing grief that befalls us and try to understand!"

God's lent child revised by Sue Johnson-Hewitt

The Four Directions and Earth Love
Fire, earth, water and air. These four directions help us to consider the interaction between all beings and the four elements of the earth. Loving our earth and all living things on it helps us to achieve good health mentally, spiritually, emotionally and physically.

Why Do Some People Not Communicate Through Mediums After They have Passed?

When we initially pass over, it is a very happy, joyful time. We are busy meeting our loved ones who have passed before us. We are taken to the Sphere that suits our needs and have time to settle in. For Spirit to communicate to someone on the Earth Plane is not as easy as we think. There are stations to go to, with experienced guides organising meetings for communication.

A medium may be chosen as their vibration suits the spirit's energy; the person on earth may be impressed upon to have a reading. For Spirit to communicate with us they have to slow down their vibrations, as theirs is a much faster frequency. If you move your hands really fast you cannot see them, this is exactly the same with the Spirit World. They are there; we just cannot see them. Communication can still be difficult, the medium may misunderstand the message, and it may seem muddled and distorted. It's like a really bad telephone line, it all depends on circumstances. For example if the medium sees a train, that could mean the person loved train spotting, or you may be going on a journey on a train, they may have been a train driver or they may have lived near a railway line. So you can see how one image can mean so many different things. If you're loved one has not been able to communicate with you through a medium or to you directly, take heart, it's not because they do not want to, but it may be very difficult at this time to do so.

We also need to remember that mediumship is not about foretelling the future. It is about proving life after death. Once you have had this, it is up to you to search and discover more about the philosophy. This is what will hold you in good stead through troubled times. Loved ones, your guides and angels cannot walk your pathway for you. They can guide as much as they can but ultimately it is down to you. It is your soul's journey not theirs. It is for you to walk it. To learn and grow! This is where the spiritual philosophy can help you. This can give you answers and understanding as to why things happen. Once we understand this we are more accepting and able to grow and move forward.

Many people sense their loved one around them. Many bereaved people will feel this or they can smell a certain odour associated with that person, this may be cigar smoke, perfume or a scent of a flower. This is definitely Spirit trying to let you know they are there, it is not in your imagination and it can prove very frustrating for Spirit when this is said. The trouble is we have very logical minds, instead of listening to our creative and intuitive side. We all need to accept out of the ordinary happenings. Our loved ones are always around us, if we send a thought, they will receive it no matter what they are doing. Ask for help and you will always receive help. This does not always come in the way we desire but in the way that is best for us and for our soul's growth.

囍

Double Happiness - Romance & Relationships
This symbol is used as a symbol of marriage, attracting romance and love. This is a traditional Chinese design. It is made up of 2 of the Chinese alphabet which means Joy. You can also place it where you can see it at all times to strengthen the connection within an existing relationship.

How Do We Understand Suicide?

Suicide is one of the saddest occurrences to happen in our lifetime, not just for the ones who have committed suicide but also for the ones who are left behind. People in this frame of mind reach such a deep depression that everything is too much, they feel they have no future. They have lost hope, so no matter what another person may say to encourage that person, they have reached such despair they are unreachable. Many people left behind feel guilty, holding the feeling that they should have done more.

At the end of the day there is always personal responsibility. We are never allowed to choose more than we cannot bear; we are all going through experiences to learn and grow. Nobody else can take on the individual lessons needed. We can be supportive, caring and compassionate but we cannot experience the lessons for other people. How many times have we commented, "They are lovely people, how come they always seem to have such bad luck?" These lovely people are also evolved souls. The further along the path you are the harder the tasks but as I have said you are never allowed to choose too much so that you cannot carry the burden. We all have inner strength that we are unaware of until such situations arise. Then we draw from within and most of us come out the other side, hopefully, stronger, wiser and more enlightened. When we do not draw from this inner strength there seems no light at the end of the tunnel. There is no connection with anything and suicide may occur.

Everyone is met by loved ones or guides; nobody is left to wander aimlessly. The only exception is if they may not want to see their loved ones initially as they may still feel distraught and disorientated. They may become Earth Bound for a short time as they may feel the need to be near people they have left behind. I have personally guided people who have taken their own life into light. Once we have talked it through they are ready to go home. There is more of this in the What Happens After Death Section on page 37.

Guides will always stay close at this time waiting for the time when the person is ready to move on. They will be taken to a calm and peaceful place to allow healing to take place, again there is no judgement only love and compassion for this soul. Many suicide victims are able to use their experience by channelling through mediums, help that might be needed for another on the Earth Plane suffering from similar distress.

The only regrets these souls might have will be for the loved ones left behind. They will feel great sorrow for the pain and anguish they have caused to others. This will be after healing has taken place and they will be able to reflect on what has happened. They will be shown what their life would have achieved if they had persisted with their life; again there is no criticism only a guiding love. We are big enough critics of ourselves.

They will have the opportunity to return back to earth, not necessarily to start all over again as some lessons would have been learnt on the way. They will, at the very least, go back to where they left off. This has to be done to continue Spiritual progress. Prayers and thoughts would be most beneficial for this soul to help them let go and move forward.

The Water Hamsa

This symbol represents the protection of water. It used in Hebrew and the Muslim faith. It monitors all the water on earth. It is also used to protect from any negative energy and when used with the evil eye it deflects any ill intent. Hamsa is the Arabic word for five which is shown in the symbol of the hand with five fingers.

WHAT ARE THE REPERCUSSIONS FROM MISTAKES MADE IN MY LIFE?

As I have already said unconditional love does not judge. The biggest critics of all are ourselves. When you initially pass back to Spirit you have a settling in period, eventually when the time is right for you, it is time to assess your life on earth. You are shown your life on earth and how your thoughts and actions affected those around you. You are shown the ripple effect from one action to another. You are shown how that person affected others around them because of what you have done or said. This is not just bad reactions but also when you gave a kind word or deed to another.

When you see how your negative reactions affected others you will be aware of their pain. You will then have the realisation of what you have done and you will instantly regret and feel full of remorse and pain for the other person. This is why we should treat others, as we would like to be treated. When we hurt another, we hurt ourselves, as we are all linked together as one. We can feel each other's pain! Your reaction from 'your heart' will beg forgiveness. Eventually forgiveness will be given but from yourself not from another and you will want to put right what has been wronged. Most of us come back within the same group of souls, which gives us a chance to repay debts owed. Roles may be reversed. Similar situations can be experienced in relationships to enable us to understand what it feels like to be on the other end of what we may have dished out in the past. This is all done in accordance with Natural Law. The scales have to be balanced out and your soul, which is part of a soul group, will need and desire to do this, as the group needs growth and progression not stagnation.

As you are going through your own personal assessment you are not alone. Higher guides will lovingly give support and understanding. They will advise and give insight into why certain things have happened, so this time is not something to fear but to be just aware of. If you are in the know now, you can start practising love to others, it is never too early or too late. It is better to try to put things right here, rather than wait until you have returned back to Spirit. Also remember though, that when we make so-called mistakes this is all part of the growing process. This is the time when we learn and maybe use the experience to aid others. There is always something constructive to look for at these times. If we were to look at the reason why the mistake occurred, for example, was it based on fear, insecurity, pride or ego, we may have the answers as to why it happened in the first place, as the saying goes "pride before a fall". Normally, so called mistakes happen when we are not listening to our inner self, we are too busy rushing around, determined to reach our goals in life, ignoring what our true selves maybe trying to tell us; "more haste, less speed" is another saying.

For most of us are oblivious to how unconnected we may have become from the Universal Energy. It will always provide for you and guide you but we are all so bogged down we shut it out. We no longer listen to our intuition, if we were to do so there would be fewer mistakes made. Our intuition is our connection to our higher self, the Universal Energy and to a higher energy. If we stopped and listened in the first place we would have more understanding as to what life is really about. As I have said though, all our so-called mistakes are learning curves to enable us to reach this understanding and connection with our true selves. So I do not think of the repercussions of our mistakes but rather the learning aspects we gain from them.

Let me give you an example of myself. I have been married four times, would this be considered mistakes in my life? I do not view it this way; I see how much each relationship has taught me. My first two marriages taught me self-worth, strength, independence and the courage to change things that were not compatible for me. I had to realise this though and through both of these relationships I learned self-awareness. I married for the wrong reasons (or so I thought). I entered these marriages because of my own insecurities and fears which I eventually overcame and moved forward. This was a weakness on my part and now hopefully I have broken away from this patterning I was following.

Everyone is our teacher; they are our tools for learning as we are for them. If I had chosen to stay in either one of the marriages, would I have failed my husbands and myself by stunting both our spiritual growths? As it is, my third marriage seems like a karmic gift. My husband Mark was a most wonderful husband. He supported me, understood me and above all loved me as I really was.

He died in 2000 after we had been together for about 6 years. The pain and grief I felt was unbelievable. My belief, this philosophy held me in good stead though as it has done throughout my life. I never once wished him back as I knew it was the right time for him to go home. I knew he was in a beautiful and wondrous place. This did not stop me grieving but again this has given me the experience, an insight to help me understand other's grief and to help them if needed.

Seven years later I was fortunate enough to have met and married another perfect man for me, Andy, who is supportive to me in different ways. I am so lucky to have found another man who enables me to have the freedom of experiences without restrictions as my freedom is so important to me. Andy totally understands and respects this. Our love for one another grows deeper and deeper as the years go on.
We all have enough love in our hearts to give to another. It is not limited.

My life now feels complete, I have no regrets about my past relationships, and I thank them with all my heart for helping me to get to this stage of my life. It has been a continuous learning cycle. I now ask you is this an achievement or a failure? I leave it to you to decide.

Spiral

This sacred symbol is to be known as the oldest to be used in spiritual beliefs. It represents fertility and the life force energy we have and our continuous journey in life. Meditate on this symbol to help you accept changes that occur in your life and flow with the tide.

Is There Free Will If Everything Is Planned?

You have decided and planned your life before you are re-incarnated. This was based on the lessons you need to learn to enable a deeper understanding for your Spiritual Growth. We all have a set pathway in life; free will comes in the way we react to life. Situations will occur where you have free will in the way you respond. If you see an old person having difficulty crossing a busy road, do you offer your help or not? The decision you make will not make any difference as such, in your daily life, but the opportunity was given to you to see if you had enough understanding and empathy for another to offer aid when needed.

These opportunities can also be given in order to pay back karmic debts. No matter how small, remember what you give out you will get back. You may have done a small unkindness to someone in a previous life and may want to make amends. So you are given the opportunity to repay back with a good deed, wiping out the debt. Opportunities come in various forms. If you saw a beggar in the street and he asks for money do you give this to him or not?

I experienced this very situation. My first reaction when this person asked me for money for a cup of tea was no, sorry. Mentally, I was thinking, if he got a job, had some purpose in his life, accepted personal responsibility, there would be no need for him to be in the position of having to ask me for money. I continued to walk on, to bank some money (ironically), but all the while I felt uncomfortable, I even slowed down. My solar plexus was feeling very jumbled (for the want of a better word). Even though in the split second I had all those thoughts about the man I also felt compassion, some form of empathy with this person, which I have never experienced before.

I went into the bank and queued up for the cashier, all the while having this mental confrontation with myself. I decided that if I could not spare this person a pound, what a sorrowful person I am. I then decided to give him two pounds, maybe to salve my conscience. I was hoping and praying he had not gone by the time I left the bank. He was not there when I went outside, I felt let down that I had obviously let an opportunity pass that was given to me to help another. I looked around and saw him walking down the road. I ran after him and just put the two pounds in his hand and off I went.

I am not suggesting we all should give to people who beg us for money, but to listen to our intuition when the need may well be genuine. I knew I had originally gone against my intuition by the way my solar plexus reacted. There was conflict within myself, maybe I had connected with his higher self and seen beyond the face of a beggar. I am not sure, but in this instance I recognised an opportunity that had come my way, listened to my intuition and followed it. This is free will. The choice was mine.

The way we react to people is down to free will, whether it be with anger, bitterness, jealousy, envy, ridicule, criticism, hatred or with compassion, empathy, understanding, forgiveness and love. Again the choice is yours. We all need to take personal responsibility for our own actions and reactions. We cannot blame others for that which they said or did which made us feel the way we do. It is because of our lack of self-worth and self love that we respond the way we do. If we were to feel unconditional love, nothing would hurt us; nothing could, as we would see beyond the mask that we wear to the world. We would see how hurt and fearful that person really was underneath all the spitefulness, anger and hatred, in fact all negative feelings. So again we do have free will in how we react to people and situations. Remember people and situations are tools to give us opportunities to reach our purpose on earth. To do this we have to climb a long road to our goal. Along the road opportunities come and go and you have the choice whether to grab them or NOT.

I will give one more example of how I used my own free will but in a different way. I went to a Spiritualist Church one Sunday evening. There was as usual a medium who conducted the service, when it came for the time for her to demonstrate clairvoyance; the medium came to me. She told me she had my Grandfather with her. Nothing unusual about that; the medium then said he was relating to a woman on the earth. I said I did not think so, as my Grandmother, his wife was also in spirit. She then said, "Hold on for a minute" and then said "he has a sister on the earth, who is unwell at the moment. I acknowledged this was true, he had a sister called Rose still here on earth. The medium then asked me to send my Granddad's love to Rose and that was that.

I then deliberated whether to write to Rose. I had only met her once and was not sure how to send her my Granddad's love, as he had passed over several years previously. After two weeks of turning it over in my mind I decided to write to Rose. I felt that as I was given this to pass on, I should do so. I had a reply within two days from Rose. She wrote that she was not into all this "weird stuff" and she did not think it was herself Granddad was referring to, but to his cousin Carrie who lived around the corner from me. Well, as you can image, I was amazed. I had moved to Bournemouth only a few months previously, not knowing I had any family links there. Rose had already telephoned Carrie and she had said it would be fine for me to ring her, which I promptly did. Carrie was a lovely lady who was also in need as her husband was ill and needed help. My Grandfather was obviously aware of this and had guided me to her even though he had taken me the long way round to get there. Maybe this was the only way to link me up with Carrie.

Carrie was also a spiritualist and used to have development circles in her home, she informed me my Grandfather had also sat in these circles. He even went into trance and had a little girl talk through him. My Grandfather had never mentioned any of this and we had had some very heavy and deep conversations in the past. I think my Nan put a stop to it all, as she did not believe in any of it. I might add though, it was this very lady, my Nan, who set me on my Spiritual Path. She was the first person to contact me through a medium with solid proof.

This led me on to make further enquiries, which I have continued to do extensively over the years and has brought me to my current awareness and belief. I thank her with love from all my heart for helping to set me on this pathway. It just goes to show how much more you understand once you pass over.

My Grandfather, Nan and their sons, one of which is of course my Father, had holidays in Bournemouth for about eleven years when they were younger. Yet no-one had mentioned to me before this fact about Carrie and I am pleased to say I now have all the photographs of that time. So, I had a choice, I could have chosen not to write the letter to Rose and would have missed the opportunity to meet Carrie. Yet I did, I had used my free will by listening to my heart not my head and risked sounding a bit odd to Rose, who gave me the chance to meet and love a wonderful lady called Carrie who has since passed back to Spirit. My Grandfather had never communicated before that Sunday evening in 1988, and the only other time since was in 2017 when my father passed over.

Lotus - From the Mud Comes the Divine

This Symbol is to give us strength when we encounter difficulties and obstacles in life. This Lotus Flower shows us how it rises from the mud at the bottom of the water and rises above the water, representing transformation. It overcomes all to reach its goal. It symbolises life, where we need gratitude, compassion, humility and forgiveness. This journey helps us to achieve this, bringing balance and learning what is important in our lives.

What Happens After Physical Death?

We all survive so-called death, as this in reality is another birth. You are first and foremost a Spiritual Being and all Spirit is part of the Universal Energy, which is a higher energy. Your spirit cannot die; this is impossible as you are indestructible. Your Physical Body is a shell surrounding you, enabling you to work and function on this Earth Plane. Your Spiritual Body motivates your Physical Body, holding all the knowledge that is required to gain experience and growth needed in this life.

Earth is a school of learning; like any school you graduate and leave to take what skills you have learnt into the world. This is exactly the same as when you die, except, there is always a place for you to go unlike a job situation where one is judged if you are competent enough. There is always the right space and level in the Spirit World for each Soul. You are assessed as to what growth has been attained, without judgement, throughout this particular lifetime. Depending on your previous lives, the speed varies in how quick you rise up the ladder. Again much the same as a job situation, nobody will be judging you but you will be continually assessed by higher guides as to when the right time will be to move forward to higher Spheres. I will explain in more detail about these levels later.

When the time for your death (re-birth) has come, your Etheric Body, which is connected to your Physical Body by a silver cord, is broken. When we are asleep we leave our body, which is an out of body experience except the majority of us do not remember this. This is called Astral

Travelling. We recollect in forms of dreams that are disjointed and most of the time does not make sense. The Etheric Body is a replica of your human body, but made of a much finer substance. This enables you to travel in Spirit freely. There are no limitations; you are able to travel the Universe if you wish. To visit other planets, to see loved ones or you may be quite happy to sit in your lounge.

When you are falling asleep and you have the sensation of jerking awake, like you have when you are falling off a kerb, your Etheric Body has returned to your body very rapidly. A loud noise or disturbance may have occurred as you were falling into a deep sleep and you were rising out of your body at that time. You then may return back into your body quickly causing a jolt. Also something may have frightened you, i.e. you were crossing the road and a lorry was coming and you thought it would run you over. Of course it cannot as your body is not physical at this time! You have allowed the only limitation to creep in, which is fear. This is our own illusion as there is nothing to fear in the Spirit World. Fear is our greatest barrier to most things; it blocks so much in our lives.

When the time has come for you to re-awaken from your sleep, a message or a pull is sent along the silver cord letting your Etheric Body know it is time to go back. This is the same as death, except the silver cord breaks and there is no need to return to your body. There will be no fear as the peace and tranquillity you feel will prevent you from feeling anything but at peace with yourself. This feeling has been experienced when people have had Outer Body Experience (OBE), to the point they do not want to return to their body.

The cord will not break until it is the correct time for our transition back to the Spirit World. No outside force has the power to disconnect the silver cords, as it is always pre-planned before you came to earth. The Spirit World works on a faster frequency, so you cannot see it with the physical eye. Mediums have developed their clairvoyance so they raise their consciousness. There are different forms of clairvoyance, but I will explain in more detail later. Through communications with mediums, Spirit slow down their frequency so the two will meet. This takes a lot of discipline, training, and you must have the right motivation to serve in this way.

The Spirit Body consists of several finer bodies that connect with your Physical Body. They operate on different levels but are all linked together to your higher self. These levels consist of Astral, Mental and Causal; again I will go into more detail later. All of these Spiritual Bodies will register every thought, word and deed to your higher self. So upon your death all information will be accessible, to enable you to evaluate all the information you have gained. No one, I repeat no one will judge you. Unconditional love does not judge. We are our own greatest critics. This reflection enables you to understand and see what has and has not been learned in this particular lifetime.

After your death the Etheric Body clings to the Physical Body, as this is the only link it has. Now the silver cord has broken there is no need for the Etheric Body, as you now have the Astral Body. The Etheric Body will begin to dissolve away as the need for it is released. Your astral body is your natural form for now. Familiar faces or guides always greet you. You are never left alone, only those who have certain beliefs and may believe that these people are the so-called devil will not acknowledge these spirits. They have been so conditioned that it may take some time for revelation and acceptance to come. These spirits can be earth-bound, as they will find comfort being around their earthly family and friends. This can also occur when the death is very quick, some people do not even realise they are dead.

There are so many reasons why people do not go into the light. It is my pleasure and honour to be able to work with these souls. To discuss what they are worried about. I ask them what is stopping them going into the light. Once I have found this out, I then talk it through with them, re-assuring them that unconditional love does not judge. (All of us will assess our own life at the right time. This will be when we will decide what experiences we wish to learn from if we choose to return to earth).

One lady murdered her husband because he beat her, cheated on her and she suffered a miscarriage through his hands. So she poisoned him with resin. Guilt was not stopping her going into the light, it was fear of seeing him waiting for her. This does not happen as you only see those you want to see.

Another lady killed her baby. She was full of shame. It became apparent that she actually was suffering with really bad post-natal depression. She died in 1923 so she had stayed earth bound all those years until 2019. She was 48 years old when she died. She was put into a mental hospital because of this depression. Back then of course there was no understanding of postnatal depression so she would not have received any of the help or support that she needed. So again I talked this through with her.

Another lady who had learning needs would not go into the light as she had embalmed her pets. She was worried that she had held her animal souls back by keeping their physical bodies. She had not married or had children so her animals were her world. Again we talked it through and she happily went into the light as all the souls I speak with do. This is my passion to help those who are scared to go into the light.

There are so many stories; too many to mention here but the above is just to give you examples of why people choose to stay earthbound. Hopefully after reading this book you will not be one of those as you will have a better understanding of life after death, Please go to my website www.f-a-c-e-life.com if you feel you have an earthbound soul in your home or building. I can do this by WhatsApp so distance is no problem if you are in another county or country. I do go personally as well when needed.

There are different Astral Levels and you will be taken to the one that suits your needs at this time. Nobody is put on a higher or lower level that is not correct for him or her.

This would make you feel very disjointed and ill at ease with the people around you because their vibration would be different from yours. I will go in more depth about these levels at a later stage.

We all incarnate for further lives as it is impossible to learn everything in one lifetime. The ultimate goal is **UNCONDITIONAL LOVE.**

We have no comprehension of this love as we base most of our relationships on conditions. We only love, like or respect a particular person if they come up to our expectations. The nearest you can get to unconditional love is the feelings you have for your children. Most would die for their children but not necessarily for spouses, parents or friends. So you see for us to attain to this level we must undertake experiences to learn. The only way to learn is to experience. We have no understanding of what certain emotions or feelings feel like unless we have completed valuable lessons.

In each lifetime we grow further and further. We also create karma on the way. These are debts we incur not just bad ones but good ones as well. What you give out, you get back. Natural Law deals with this in which you cannot cheat or fool. The scales must come into balance, so we incur debts from past lives as well as in the present life. We are given opportunities to clear our debts, whether to help an elderly person across the road or stand by people when in need. We also have free will so it is down to personal responsibility whether or not to grab the opportunities as they come.

The only way to learn is to experience certain situations which enable us to gain insight and wisdom into what that lesson may have taught us, hopefully for the better of mankind as a whole. If you are kind, thoughtful, compassionate and honest to others then your level in the Spirit World will be higher than those who are uncaring, dishonest, selfish and violent. Then again if we were all perfect souls we would not be here on the earth, there would be no need. So the art is to try and recognise our shortcomings and work on improving our reaction to people and situations. Above all learn to love yourself. Until you have achieved this, how can you really love others as we are all as one anyway!

The Triade, Triskele, or Triple Spiral

This is a Celtic symbol. It represents our time on earth, our time in spirit and reincarnation. It can relate to the elements of earth and water, also to the sky, our body, mind and spirit. It is a continuous line, showing a fluid movement of time.

WHAT ARE THE DIFFERENT PSYCHIC ABILITIES?

There are different forms of Divination to use with our Psychic and mediumistic abilities. Some of the different forms of divination/psychic abilities come in the form of Psychometry, Tarot or playing cards, tea leaf reading and runes. Anything can be used as a tool. I have used, shells, feathers, coloured cards to name but a few. The mediumistic abilities are clairvoyance, clairsentience, clairaudience, clairgustiance and clairolfactory. I have only written a very brief description on the above as there is already plenty of literature specialising in these subjects.

Psychometry

This is a gift in which a person can develop by tuning into people's objects. They can pick up the vibrations the object has absorbed from the person. Your Auric Field is impressed on the object, which the psychic tunes into, enabling them to do a reading. The longer you have had the item the stronger the impression of you will have been absorbed. This is not linking to the Spirit World; most people have this ability if they practice enough.

Tarot Cards or Playing Cards

Each pack of Tarot Cards has a small booklet describing the meaning of each card. These cards are used as guidance and intuition plays a big part in this. It depends on the development of the card reader on which level the reading goes, some are more in depth than others. You can also ask yes and no questions with this type of divination.

Crystal Ball

As with the Tarot Cards, the crystal ball is just a tool to enable us to tune into our higher selves. The crystal ball is really just a focus point as it can prove unnerving for clients if the medium continually looks over their shoulder when talking about or describing Spirit. A plain bowl of water with a dark background will do just the same job. This is called Scrying, when staring into the crystal ball, your eyes go slightly out of focus and forms may appear in the ball. Sometimes symbolic signs may be shown which the medium can interpret.

Clairvoyant

A clairvoyant is a person who is able to raise their consciousness to attune to the Spirit World so contact can be made. Sometimes it can prove difficult for the medium to translate what is being impressed or said. This is where misunderstandings come in, as none of us are perfect. Clairvoyance is where the medium receives communication through pictures impressed from Spirit. They can be a very strong, clear picture or be slightly faded or distorted; it all depends on the two-way communication. Spirit may be just starting to learn how to communicate this way, so it may be weak or disjointed. It's not always the medium's fault. Patience and discipline is required to do this service. A developing clairvoyant will build up their own interpretation of symbols or scenes, which may represent the same thing to them. This is a form of communication that has been worked out between the medium and their guides. This is mostly learnt in developing circles. It may take years for a medium's abilities to develop, so again, it takes a lot of commitment, time and discipline to learn and use this gift and you must have patience. Interpretation is very hard at times as mentioned before in the train example.

Clairaudience

Clairaudience is to hear Spirit. Some mediums see and hear Spirit, this can be like someone talking into your ear or just a voice talking or sometimes even shouting (to make sure they are being heard), to you inside your head. You know this is not you as it is a totally different voice. Try and hear your own voice talking in your head now, it is very difficult to imagine this. So you will have no difficulty in knowing this voice has come from outside of you. This can prove to be a very accurate way of communication, as this can be very clear and detailed. Again it is like a telephone line, so some distortion can occur, names etc., may not always be so clear. It all depends on the development of the medium and the experience of the person in Spirit communicating abilities. It can also come in as thoughts in your head. Words may come into your mind. You may think this is you but it is not. They will use the way you would relate to words to communicate. This is quite common.

Clairolfactory and Clairgustiance

Clairolfactory is the ability to experience smells. This can come in the smell of the persons perfume, aftershave, odour, flower, smoking, grass, baking, a hobby or place of work, or any other memory links.

Clairgustiance is the ability to experience taste. This could be the taste of the persons favourite meal, drink, cigarettes or pipe, sweetness, sourness, bitterness, salty, spicy and even mouth wash to name a few.

Clairsentience

Clairsentience is when we sense things. This is using your sixth sense. You seem to be picking something up, whether it is a warning, or something that did not feel quite right with a certain situation or with another person. We can all sense when something does not feel right in some way. When a medium works in this way, they can be temporarily given the sensation of a type of illness or disabilities the person in Spirit may have passed over with or had during their life time on earth. They may also be able to pick up the feeling of any ailments you personally or someone around you may be suffering. Many mediums are able to receive communication by developing two or all three of the above Psychic gifts to enable a more detailed reading.

Runes

There are 25 Runes that you 'cast' to predict the future.

You can ask yes and no questions with them and they can be very accurate. The Runes come in many forms i.e. stones, wood, crystals, cards and they are based on Viking mythology. A lot of men prefer to work with Runes as their energy is masculine.

Peace - Peaceful Waters Stimulate Creativity
Balance between opposing forces creates peace and beauty. This Chinese symbol represents the peaceful flow of waters that calm, heal and inspire.

What Happens to Animals When They Die?

Everything is connected with the Universal Energy of Love. Your pet animal will always be connected to you through this love. They will be waiting to greet you when the time for your transition arises. Again, when you are asleep you will be with your pet whenever you want. All animals are cared for in the Spirit World. There are no limitations. Food, water and warmth are all unnecessary in the Spirit World, so freedom comes to mind for us as well as your pets. There is no time in the Spirit World, so your pet will not forget you, their memory will be fresh as when they passed over. As with us humans, animals come from a group soul. Individual animals pour back their experience into one pool to make a whole. The same goes for wild animals, when they have not had individual human love they merge with their group. This group is forever growing and moving forward. The fear of humans must be removed which is where we play an important part in expressing love for all animals.

Many animals will hang around after death to try and bring comfort to their owners. Their love has no boundaries so they will wait patiently for your permanent return back to spirit. Eventually the time will come when the animal will need to return to their group soul. By this time your understanding of this will enable you to let go with love.

Earth Medicine Wheel - Harmony and Earth Peace

This represents the four elements of the fire, earth, water and air. This is a Native American symbol that shows peace and love between all.

Meditate on this symbol to help all mankind and for personal strength and power.

How Will I Know Which Partner To Choose If I've Had More Than One?

The rules are different in the Spirit World compared to our earthly conditions. Marriage is a man made institution in which commitment is proven this way. In the Spirit World this is not required, as love is the bond that is needed to link to one another. When we return back to the Spirit World we eventually release our emotional needs and insecurities as they diminish. So what you desired here on earth as a person may no longer be needed anymore.

Most couples if they wish to stay together will until the time comes when each individual needs to follow separate pursuits. This will happen naturally and both parties will be ready to do this, although you are never really completely parted as you can link to anyone at any time. Jealous feelings no longer rise up as all emotional insecurities that we were driven by on earth are released, so this enables us to let go easily and peacefully with love.

If you have had more than one partner and you are worried about which one you should be with, do not worry. You will feel drawn to the right partner as long as this feeling is returned. Former partners will understand as they will already know what is right for everybody. As the rules are different there is the possibility of living as a small group, as jealousy does not arise, only mutual love. Remember there are no limitations; marriage is no longer an issue in the Spirit World, just freedom to love. Everything is on a higher level and that includes the type of love we feel and

express.
Natural law balances everything out accordingly; life in Spirit offers so much more satisfaction and completion that the desire for one person will eventually fade away. We will be able to express our love, which is giving freedom to another. Treat others, as we would like to be treated while we can whilst we are on earth.

If you have no wish to be with former partners than this will be so, nobody will be hurt or offended. As I have already explained love is expressed on a higher level that means the ability to let go freely. So just enjoy this life with your partner in the NOW but try and self analyse and make sure the relationship foundations are not because of your insecurities and fears as a lot of relationships unfortunately are based on these feelings.

Gayatri Yantra

The Illumined Mind and Universal Knowledge -
This symbol represents inner wisdom. It helps to enhance the ability in your intellect and spirituality. The Gayatri Mantra helps to make the right choices by empowering truth. It vocalises wisdom about all life on earth and all the elements.

WHY DOES A HIGHER ENERGY ALLOW SO MUCH SUFFERING IN THE WORLD?

First and foremost a higher energy does not order that pain, destruction, fear and terror to be put on mankind. Humans do! We all have free will and over the centuries we have created karma worldwide. What you put out you get back. This is Natural Law balancing everything out. A higher energy has not created all the negativity in our world. We are the ones who have abused our free will through so-called progression. In this process we have learnt to react with greed, anger, bitterness, resentment, cruelty, jealousy, all negative reactions to our experiences that we have created ourselves. We have abused the Mother Earth, which affects the elements so when we have earthquakes, tornadoes, hurricanes, we wonder why all this is happening and why higher beings are allowing this to happen. Maybe this is Natural Law trying to clear out the clutter and chaos that the world has created. It is always noticeable how through traumatic circumstances everybody pulls together, looks after and cares for other people. Going back to roots! Unfortunately we need a kick up the bum to remind us.

As there is no such thing as death, people who have passed over in these circumstances were meant to die at this time. These people needed to experience this type of death for whatever reason. Again, we do not remember what we may have been or done in previous lives, we may need to have a violent death to understand what this entails but none of us has all the answers. How often do we hear people say they were supposed to be on that train or plane that crashed and they were blocked from getting on that transport at that point. It was because it was not their time to pass over.

Most of our emotional pain is self-created, not a higher energy's way as it is our choice of reaction to our experiences that controls us. A higher energy has given us a pure heart to love and to give, if we choose not to do so, when we go against our true selves, our higher self, pain and confusion reigns. Personal responsibility needs to be learnt; we are so busy blaming someone else or a higher energy for our reactions. If we choose to react angrily or violently, this is not a higher energy's way. A higher energy does not sit up there throwing stones at us, it sends pure love. We are so bogged down with emotional baggage we do not open ourselves to receive it. So Personal Responsibility is the key. If we accept this, we are halfway there in accepting life with a warm and open heart.

I will refer to another of my favourite poems, this is a famous poem called Footprints.

Footprints

*One night a man had a dream. He dreamed he was
walking along the beach with the Lord
Across the sky flashed scenes from his life.
For each scene he noticed two sets of footprints in the
sand: one belonging to him and the other to the Lord.*

*When the last scene of his life flashed before him
He looked back at the footprints in the sand. He
noticed that many times along the path of his life
there was only one set of footprints. He also noticed
that it happened at the very lowest and saddest times
in his life.*

*This really bothered him and he questioned the Lord
about it. "Lord, you said that once I decided to follow
you, you would walk with me all the way.
But I have noticed that during the most troublesome
times in my life, there is only one set of footprints. I
don't understand why, when I needed you most you
would leave me".*

> *The Lord replied "My son, my precious child.
> I love you and I would never leave you.
> During your times of trial and suffering, when
> you see only one set of footprints,
> it was then that I carried you."*

Author Unknown

Before you come to earth you decide your path, you will know what experiences you need for your Spiritual Growth. A higher energy does not decide this, as unconditional love does not judge, just gives understanding and support. Higher guides, Angels and yourself, discuss any lessons that you may have decided your soul needs at this time. We do not learn when we are in happy times, we learn and grow when we are down on our knees and we drag ourselves up, dust ourselves down and carry on. We draw from inner strength, which is always in supply. These experiences enable us to be a more compassionate, forgiving, loving soul to others, which equips us to help others when they are in need.

A higher energy's love is so pure it has given free will to allow us to grow. If we were to shut our children in a room to protect them from the big wide world we would not be helping their progress; we would be hindering and blocking their growth. We try to equip them with knowledge they may need in the big wide world. All we can do is just let them go but be there when they need us. This is the same as a higher energy, it is always there for us if only we would sit in the quiet and listen.

When I look back on my own life I could have chosen to blame a higher energy for all the lessons I had experienced since childhood. I had an alcoholic Mother throughout my childhood, (but I am proud to say that she has been sober since the late 1980s). I had a controlling father which carried on into my first two marriages. A pattern I obviously followed into adult life. I was bullied all the way through school, even up to when I had my first child in hospital and this carried on until I was 34 years old. I did not really have any friends or boyfriends until I was 16 years old due to my home life. I could go on but there is no need to at this time. Now, I realise that I have chosen my parents for the very lessons they have taught me. There was obviously a karma link as well.

To enable me to be a therapist of any worth I had to have experiences that would enable me to relate and empathise with other people's suffering. Again as I have said so many times, unless you have experience you have no understanding. If I had had an idyllic childhood, no problems, cocooned from life, married happily, again without any real problems in life how could I possibly relate to others? In fact, how could I be teaching Spiritual Philosophy if I had had no experience of adapting the philosophy to my past and daily life? I do not have any regrets about my upbringing. I am grateful that this has equipped me for the work I have to do. I could have chosen to blame a higher energy for a bad lot, but instead I see how positive and constructive my life has been to date. I accept personal responsibility for the choices I made for my Spiritual Growth.

Taijitu

This Taoist sign represent Yin and Yang, The feminine and masculine energy within us all, also the darkness and light in life. Knowledge and ignorance! The yin is the emotional, sensitive, passive side and the yang is the dominant and practical side. We need both to bring balance within us.

Why Do Some People Have Harder Lives Than Others?

Our lifetime on earth is like acting in a play. You choose the script and the part you are to act. This could be the hero, the victim, a poor person, a rich person, or a famous person; the choice is yours. You choose your parents, your birth date, your death date and even your birth name. You do this with every life you have on earth. This enables you to complete all lessons that are required. It is more like going to college and then university. There are set courses that you may need to complete, to help you with your tasks. Like tutors and lecturers we have here, we have our guides, angels and higher ones in spirit guiding us, advising how much we are able to achieve. This will make sure we do not choose too much so it is not too much to bear. If we did everyone would commit suicide. We need our play times. Earth is a school for learning, always expanding and growing.

If someone else's life does not include so much suffering, they may have chosen to come back to earth to teach or heal. Everyone's level of tolerance is different, what may seem hard for another may be easy for you. So everyone's karma is suited for individual needs, as the saying goes unless you have walked in the other person's shoes you have no understanding of what that person has suffered.

The simpler the needs the fewer burdens we have. However so called progression has created in us the desire for material things that we would not consider if we lived a simpler life where our only worries would be food and shelter.

Indian tribes lived simply; they catered for their needs, no more or less. They made wigwams, hunted for food, made their own clothes and jewellery. Their life was more fulfilled than ours, as they were more in touch with nature's law. They worked with nature rather than against it. This is one of the lessons we need to learn. We choose a life, which will give us the best tuition we need. Many of you will say I would not have chosen the life I have but you are responding with your earthly mind not your Spiritual Mind; your higher self is aware of all the lessons you need. We cannot remember so we get bogged down with all our problems, we are no longer clear-sighted. We are unable to tune into our higher self. We no longer listen to our intuition, which is our best teacher of all. This is our very own tutor who has all the answers.

The life you have chosen has been set up by you yourself to present opportunities to learn and grow, which can only be done through experiences. The situation is not important; this is only the tool to bring this experience to you. Your reaction is the most important aspect. The situation is there to evoke your reactions, to see how much you have learnt. If you have not, the same situation will keep arising in different ways until you have learnt the lesson that this is trying to teach you. You have an agreement with your guardian angels that certain lessons must be learnt in this lifetime. Your guardian angel's job is to ensure that you get these lessons otherwise you are not going to be too pleased when you go back to Spirit and you have not achieved what you set out to do. So look and accept all experiences with an open heart. This is giving you the opportunity for wisdom and understanding, and will enable you to draw closer and closer to your ultimate goal - UNCONDITIONAL LOVE.

Om - Sacred Sound of Creation
This sound is by which earth was created. Om represents the past, present and future. When chanted we blend all time as one. This is to help us to connect to our higher selves and to source.

WHY CAN I NOT REMEMBER PAST LIVES?

If we all knew the answers before we began studying for an exam it would be a pointless exercise. The whole point of studying is to learn discipline, patience and endurance as well as to have knowledge. What would be gained if you already had all the answers? We all need to stretch ourselves that bit more to achieve things in life, this way we appreciate our lives at lot more. Your higher self has all the memories of your past lives. We do have the ability to tap into these memories, through hypnotherapy or they may come in forms of dreams or in meditation. You would need to be on a level of deep understanding to be able to recollect these memories otherwise they would not give any great comfort.

There are courses that are run by experienced teachers who are qualified in past life regression who can help you tap into your previous lives. This may help you release any fears or insecurities related to a past life that may be affecting you now. We can also be affected by our past life ancestors. Their acts and beliefs can be passed down into our cell memory. So when we delve into this subject it needs to be done with the right tuition and guidance. It is a very interesting subject with great results if done in the right way.

Most of us have lived through many centuries. We have seen so called witches burned at the stake, people being hanged and beheaded for very small crimes that is if any crime had been committed at all. Some of us may well have been the accused that have suffered these atrocities or could have well have been in the crowd, jeering and encouraging these slaughters. We now look back and see these actions as barbaric. We have grown and evolved so much through time.

Many of us return to earth with souls whom we were related to in previous lives. The roles may be reversed, father, son, mother, daughter, sister, brother etc. In family relationships we create a lot of our good and not so good karma, although all karma is constructive. Karma is just a chance to learn and grow not to be feared. Some situations may have to be experienced first-hand, on what could be on the other side of the fence to have a deeper understanding, empathy and compassion.

You may have been an alcoholic mother or father in a previous life and have chosen to be born into a family of the same situation; you are the child this time not the parent. There is no point remembering all this or the relationships you had with people in the past lives as this would effect your judgement of them in the NOW. This would be of no benefit to you or to them. We all have an important role to play in each other's lives. Each one of us can be each other's teacher. If we remembered a friend in this lifetime as an enemy in another life how would we react to this? It would affect the whole plan of interaction between you both. This friend may need the opportunity to put right what may have been wronged before, but your judgement may prevent this if the understanding is not completely developed.

Pentagram

This symbol represents the 4 elements of fire, earth, water and air. The top point means the spirit. The circle represents protection, eternity and infinity, the cycles of life and nature.

WILL I MEET ALL MY LOVES ONES IN THE SPIRIT WORLD?

As people are dying it is quite common for those around to hear the person calling out names of loved ones who have already passed over. Some even speak of seeing loved ones around their bed waiting for the transition. This is quite true although unfortunately people put this down to being delirious.

Your loved ones will always meet you, as all of them will know in advance of your birth date back to the Spirit World. No matter which level these people are on, the bond of love will always connect with you and they would have received a message advising of your arrival. Many will have spent most of your life guiding and helping you as much as possible. You are never completely separated from your loved ones. It is just at this point you are unable to see or hear them until you have developed these gifts. It is within all us to have this ability. You do meet them when you are asleep but as I have said previously most will not remember these meetings.

There will be many people you will meet from past lives that you have no recollection of in this life. You will meet your Guides and High Ones when the time is right. There are no limitations in the Spirit World. You are able to communicate with anybody you wish, even if that someone is serving in some other area, that person can still telepathically respond at the same time. There are various aspects of our selves so we are able to do more than one thing at a time. When we meet people we will see them as we remembered them, as this is the illusion we have created of them. Eventually this will pass as awareness grows and we see that person in their true light, literally!

Dharma Wheel -
The 8 fold path to enlightenment

This is a Buddhist tradition where the 8 spokes on this wheel represent 8 pathways. Which are:- right intention, right speech, right view, right action, right livelihood, right effort, right mindfulness and right concentration. This symbol is used to strengthen devotion in mind, spiritually, emotionally and physically, bringing balance in all ways.

WHAT IS QUALITY OF LIFE?

Quality of Life is the most important part of our time here on earth, as this is part of the growing process. How we react to life is what governs the quality of how we live, whether that is mentally, spiritually or physically, in fact all three are inter-linked. If one of these aspects of one's self is out of balance, the whole of you becomes unbalanced. Everything works together. If we become emotionally upset we then get a reaction within the physical body creating ill health, we did not link into our higher self, or our intuition. If we had, the emotional upset would not have occurred in the first place, as we would have had a deeper understanding and knowledge to enable us to react in a loving way. Instead we react from our insecurities and fears.

Then again, if we all have reached this level we would not need to return to earth to learn this understanding, unless you came back to serve and help human kind in some way. Most of us carry emotional baggage, which mainly stems from our childhood, which we take into adult life. We all have our insecurities and fears, which affect the quality of our lives as most reactions are based on these foundations.

Some people may be more materially money minded due to a poor upbringing or a rich upbringing. There are no rules. This would reflect how insecure we feel inside so we over compensate by displaying material goods to give the impression of how successful we really are. Do not get me wrong, there is nothing wrong with having nice things around us to enable us to live in comfort. It only becomes an imbalance when it becomes so important to you to portray this type of life style, when maybe you cannot really afford to do so or just do it to impress others.

Again our insecurities affect our relationships. If we were continually criticised or bullied in our childhood, we may grow into adulthood with both low self-worth, anger and be defensive to others. This again affects our quality of life. How can we interact on a balanced level with these feelings? It is how we view our experiences that govern our Quality of Life. All the baggage we carry affects our reactions, we are frightened we may get hurt or used or we allow ourselves to get hurt or used. So all our emotional insecurities affect the quality of our lives which then starts to affect our physical body, we then become even more limited. Our quality of life goes down even more. When we become unwell in our physical body, there is an emotion behind every ailment.

I recommend The Bodymind Workbook by Debbie Shapiro and Heal Thyself by Louise Hay which will explain the emotion behind the illness and more detail about your disease with yourself.

Our body talks to us all the time, telling us when there is an imbalance within ourselves. Most of us do what is expected of us; we have grown up in a society that has taught us that if we think of ourselves we are being selfish. This is where most of our problems stem from. We all behave accordingly in every aspect of our lives, whether this is with our friendships, parents, partners, employment or learning environment. This is governed by other people's expectation of each and every one of us. How can we love others if we do not love ourselves? By putting ourselves first, learning to say no when we want to, does not imply we are being selfish. I am not saying that we relinquish our responsibilities of life, only that our attitude to these responsibilities could help to make life a lot easier for us. We tend to do things to please others rather than not at all. Nobody wants to be disliked but on the other hand what price do all of us pay just to be liked superficially or to look good? Not all of us express the real us, we are afraid that maybe nobody will love or like the real us. When we give freely with love this is the true self. When we give begrudgingly, with resentment, anger or even in guilt, this does not go hand in hand with our actions. Your body responds to this two-way pull, imbalance occurs.

The art of quality of life is true honesty and acceptance of our-selves. You will then find the love from your heart will flow freely and balance will be restored to the body. The emotional physical and spiritual part of you will then interlink on a harmonious level.

The Cross

The symbol of the cross represents Christianity. This depicts the crucifixion of Jesus. Many people make the sign of the cross as an act of faith and dedication.

WHAT IS THE DIFFERENCE BETWEEN GUIDES, SPIRIT HELPERS AND GUARDIAN ANGELS?

When we are born we have one guide who will stay by our side until the day we die. It can be an Indian, Egyptian, Chinese or a guide from any origin. The reason so many are told they have an Indian Guide is because they were the most spiritually aware whilst on earth. They were in tune with nature and its elements. They lived simply to their needs rather than for greed, yet they also knew of hardship, sacrifices, responsibility and duty. They are protectors of our emotions. They come through very strongly when people are going down new pathways in life or when we have reached a crossroads. Sioux Indian Guides work with a lot of mediums and the Indians guide us with astral travel. Egyptian Guides help with psychic development and our intuition. They also help those whose interest lies in astrology. They help a lot with logical thought processes. Chinese Guides draw close to those whose interest lies in the medical profession or those in complimentary therapies. They also help us when we are studying. Nuns draw close to those who are nursing or caring for people, they help us to develop patience with others. They also help us to try to develop inner peace. Monks draw close to us at times when we feel alone or in doubt about our beliefs. They help us to develop the art of meditation and inner peace. If we can stop and listen then they are able to guide us in a wise and quiet way.

We do have different guides at different stages of our lives. Your main guide will always remain with you but at times you may need the help of others with different types of experience and knowledge. There are also your Spirit Helpers, which may come in the form of family, friends and those from previous lives, which you have forgotten at this time. Our families need to have the opportunity to serve and help mankind, to help themselves evolve, move up rather than stagnate. When we are in need we must ask our guides and helpers for help. They can only help us so far as we have free will, so they need our permission to give us that little bit more to help us on our way. I have often heard people say 'I do not like to ask, it doesn't seem right.' Oh, how frustrating this is for all our dear loved ones in Spirit. We are being selfish really in thinking along these lines.

Our Spirit friends need to have opportunities to repay debts, to serve and help us to help their own Spiritual Growth. To enable them to express love we need to accept this love, not block it. So we are not only hindering ourselves but also hindering others in their growth because of our misunderstanding of asking for love and guidance. It is a two-way flow of energy; allow this to flow between our Spirit World and us. Ask and you will receive, not necessarily in the way you want but in the way it is required for your Spiritual Growth. If you have a question, ask and it will be answered in some form. You may get the answer straight away or it may come within months or even years. The answer will always come at the right time; we may not always be ready to receive the answer at the time of asking. Maybe we need to experience a little, to have full understanding of what the answer may be. We need to learn patience; we want all the answers NOW.

One thing we cannot do is force, hurry or bully Spirit in conforming to us. We have to learn to wait, for the right time will come.

Guardian Angels are on a totally different Sphere. They have never had to come to earth; their Etheric bodies are made of even finer substance than ours. These angels are to guard as well as guide you. When you decide that you are ready to return to earth, it is with your Guardian Angels that you sit down and discuss what lessons you need to learn whilst on earth. This will help you decide on what certain experiences you need to have to enable you to have a deeper understanding of humanity as a whole. This will give you the opportunity to repay back debts you may have incurred from previous lives. This enables natural law to balance everything out. Now, a lot of people while on earth will often be heard to say 'I would not have chosen this life, it has been terrible. I will not be coming back again.' This is because they are reacting with their earthly mind rather than their Spiritual Mind. They cannot see the whole plan; they only see a fragment, which makes no sense to them at all. It is like a jigsaw puzzle, until you see the whole you are unsure what the finished product will look like, so you take your time, putting all the pieces together using the picture on the lid as a guide. Your guidance to this puzzle of life is yourself, your intuition. We have forgotten why we originally came to earth. Your Guardian Angel's love for you is so pure and it is their job to make sure you are able to achieve what you set out to do. We may try to run away but we will still run head on to the same problems. It may come dressed up in a different scenario, but nevertheless it will be still the same content.

Your Guardian Angel will always step in and put the lesson in front of you. If you do not learn the first time, they will give it to you again and again until you finally learn. How many times have we said of someone 'will they never learn?' Yes, eventually, how long it takes is down to the individual.

If you did not experience anything or learn anything while you were here on earth you would soon be jumping up and down when you went back to the other side. You would be asking your Guardian Angels what were they doing and feeling what a waste of time it all was. It would be like going to school and leaving having learned absolutely nothing, being unable to read, write, count, talk or knowing how to interact with other people etc. We would all be wondering what on earth all our teachers were doing all that time. It is the same with our Guardian Angels; they are our teachers to whom we look for guidance and learning for our growth. They will also record all your thoughts, words and actions throughout your life. They work for the laws of karma. What you put out, you will get back. This works positively as well as negatively, another good reason to watch how we think and what we say to others. If we treat others how we ourselves would like to be treated we would not have much to worry about in life would we?

Hexagram or Star of David - Union of Opposites

The overlay of the up-pointing and down-pointing triangles within this star represents the connection between God and man and the union between male and female. It also can be seen as the sacred chalice, pouring unconditional love down to us on earth from the downward triangle and us receiving blessings from above from the pointing up triangle.

WHAT ARE THE DIFFERENT ASTRAL PLANES?

The best way to describe these planes/levels is like in an office block. This office block has never ending floors. It just keeps going up and up. On each floor shall we say, are departments with different aspects in each one. As it goes higher we would not be able to comprehend what this may entail. So I am only going to concentrate on 7 floors.

Each Plane is a mirror image of the stage of development we have reached at the point of death. We live on the plane that suits us at that point of time. We could not dwell higher or lower, as it would feel most uncomfortable. We need to be with souls of like mind, the same mentality, at the same stage of development. This does not mean you cannot move higher or lower because you can for short periods of time. You may be allowed to experience the higher spheres but would not be able to stay long as the energy may prove to be too strong and the light too bright.

You may move down to the lower levels, which many do to help souls evolve, to try and help them look beyond their own entrapment of misery. They will eventually see the light, as no-one is left behind. There is always love, support and understanding to help these misguided souls and show them their misery is only of self-making. Like I have said the different levels are a mirror image so all around will be of like minds. This is why it is needed for more developed souls to give help and try to break down the barriers these souls have put around themselves. You must remember though, these people will not realise their misery; to them it will seem normal. As you were on earth so you will be when initially you go back to Spirit until a deeper understanding is learnt.

First Plane

The first floor of the Astral Level is the exact copy of the Earth Plane. Many people will go here, as it will be somewhere they recognise. On this level, it is a bit like going upstairs in a house, and you can hear everything downstairs and are able to see everything on earth as it is. Everything is exactly the same. If you want to eat, drink or smoke you only have to think it and you have it. You can only experience things you have knowledge of. There is no point in thinking you want a brandy if you have never tasted this whilst on earth as you will have no recollection of what the taste would be like. Everything you want you can have, the only trouble with this is it will get boring after a while. There is nothing to strive for anymore. No progression. As you move about this level there are pubs, shops, everything that you would envisage that copies the earth plane.

If you decide to have a game of darts, the arrows will go exactly where you wish as you have thought it. If you have a game of chess, you will always win because when you play, the goal is to win and that is what you are projecting. What you may wish for you can have, the only problem is the souls on this level may not be that spiritually evolved if they choose to stay on this Plane. This is where the stigma of Ouija boards comes in. Many people will play this for fun, many are drinking while doing this, and also young people may dabble in this while their hormones are haywire. All bad news. Like will attract like. If you do this for the wrong reasons you will attract those on the lower levels to you. If you do it in truth and love you will draw those from a higher level to you. Unfortunately this goes unrecognised and now has a bad name. If people were taught and guided, these things would be unable to happen.

Many spirits have come through foretelling deaths, accidents and bad fortune but they would be unable to come through if the energy were full of love and a desire for truth. We should not have a mundane desire of everyday living, although you do need to establish an element of proof but for wisdom, knowledge and teachings of what could really help us in our daily life. Saying that though, I would not advise pupils to dabble in these things unless with a developed teacher. I have only mentioned the above to dispel the myth that it is all bad. As with everything there is a good side and a bad side.

Many will just pass through this first level to the level that suits them. You may spend as short a time or as long as you want on each level as you pass through. There are no rules that say you must move up; only when you are ready your soul will stir you if it feels you are staying too long. It will know you need to progress but again it will be at the right time for you.

Second plane

This is the Plane most will settle on for a while. It is about a mile above Plane One. You can still hear everything on earth but it is in the far distance, so you are still connected mentally to earth if you are not ready to completely let go. Everything happens gradually, slowly, at each one's pace. There are shops, hotels, churches, beautiful houses and colourful gardens as you move around this level. Unlike level one where everything is an exact copy of everything on earth, on this level everything is constructed through thought and imagination.

If you were an interior designer on earth there is no limitation in Spirit. You can create all that you wish; with materials you may have yearned for on earth as well as materials we have no knowledge of at this time. Many people will still need this talent, even in the Spirit World, if their imagination is not on the same par in this field. The same goes for architects; again there are no limitations. They are able to design whatever they wish to be able to express beauty that may have been impossible on earth.

There are no cars as there is no need for them. You only have to visualise where you want to go and whom you wish to be with and you are there. There is no need for money but again with thought form if the need is still there you can still exchange money with others of the same mind in shops, hotels etc. If you want to stay in luxury you may but, eventually, your soul will urge you to move on. You will eventually get bored and will need something with more substance, more depth, the need for more Spiritual Knowledge, but in the meantime it is for you to enjoy, relax and for your Spirit to recharge up and explore all the different departments. Some, I am sure are beyond our understanding whilst on earth. Exciting!

Third Plane

There are many open places on this level. Beautiful fields with trees and flowers, there are large houses dotted about. This is where painting is inspired; again this is done by thought form. Groups of people will get enjoyment in watching artists paint. The artist is able to express himself without any limitation. The colours will not be as on earth, they will be more vibrant, alive, and in fact indescribable to us on earth. You won't just see the art but you will feel the passion and love that has been put into this painting.

This is the level for the learning of the arts. There are musicians and famous conductors. As with the art, the same with the music. You will not just hear the musician, you will feel every vibration from that note they play into your being. Famous and experienced musicians are more than willing to teach and pass on their knowledge. There are many halls of learning which cover every subject we can think of and more that we are at this moment unaware of.

There is no day or night, so sleep is not required. When we are enjoying what we are doing times flies by but in spirit there is no time. We do not have to stop, we can continue for however long we wish. You do not get tired or feel weary; you have no other responsibilities to tend to. There is no limitation, just to allow your soul to flourish, to expand, and to be alive. There are no negative thoughts on this level, as we are unable to hide our thoughts, as everyone would know what you are thinking. You can have whatever you wish, so there is no reason to feel envious of anyone else. Here people can be themselves, there is no need for masks, and you can be who you truly are.

Fourth Plane

This is a more mental than physical plane. There is less physical activity; mental discussion is more in the line here. This is usually done by thought rather than by speaking the words. This can be about evolutionary problems, science, formation of theories, and discussion on the angelic kingdom, Devas and nature spirits. It is less material here; these people are more spiritually evolved. There is contact with Devas Spirits who play an important role on earth.

Around all our trees and plants are what are called Nature Spirits. These tend and nurture all living things. When we are talking to plants we are also talking to them, asking them to help the plant in the way it may need with love and care. Nature Spirits help the vibration of Mother Earth. They can create the most beautiful music to help raise the vibration. Each note has a vibration of its own to help create harmony and tranquillity. Their interest is only of nature and its elements; they have no desire to have contact with human beings. That is why it is not commonly known about them while on earth.

Fifth Plane

This is where Doctors and Specialists join together to pool together their ideas and experience, to help find new answers to earth's medical problems and to impress to those on earth this knowledge to help mankind. Economic problems are discussed when a crisis occurs in our world. People on this level will deliberate, to find answers to these problems and again try to impress those who have the authority like world leaders to act upon the conclusion that may be required. For example, when there are food crises within our world thoughts are formed from spirit to help cultivate new ideas, helping countries to resolve food problems.

All of these departments are on all levels but vary in degree of experience and knowledge. The same as on earth! I will give you an example by using different levels of nursing. This is just an analogy to explain how it changes as we go up. I have not included all the duties our amazing nurses do. This is to help you to relate to the different levels. Each are important in their own way.

Level 1-2
Nursing assistants aid qualified nurses by bathing, dressing, feeding patients amongst other caring duties..

Level 3
Licensed practical Nurses take blood pressure, inserting catheters, may start IV drips amongst many other nursing duties.

Level 4
Registered nurses are responsible for recording patient medical history, monitoring symptoms and medical equipment, administering medicines and collaborating with doctors. Again there is much more responsibility involved including other duties not mentioned.

Level 5
Advance practice registered nurse. They can perform all of the duties of an RN as well as more extensive tasks like

ordering and evaluating test results, referring patients to specialists and diagnosing and treating ailments.

You can see how more experienced the nurses are when they go up a level. This is the same with all walks of life.

Sixth Plane

The sixth level is a very quiet peaceful level. This is where you are able to meditate. This is the place where you require total silence, so people know to always keep their voices quiet. It is a bit like a hermit state where you are able to contemplate, still your mind, to have total control over your being. By the time you have reached this level you would have reached the state of mind which is needed here. You will only go to this level if you require it. This is the preparation for the mental levels that you are now drawing nearer to.

Seventh Plane

This is the last level before the Mental Planes. This level is similar to the Sixth Level, where you meditate in preparation for your second death. This is where you let go of your Astral Body. This is totally painless; it is like going to sleep and waking up in another Sphere. Your guide accompanies you to ensure you are not fearful in any way. It is just a natural progression a bit like going from child to adult. Your Astral Body is no longer required in the Mental Level; everything is done by thought. The Astral Body left behind will eventually disintegrate, just the same as our Physical Body does. You are met just as you were when you first went back to Spirit from earth. It is like starting school in the infants (Astral), then onto the Juniors (Mental), and then onto Senior School. (Causal)

There will be many friends and loved ones on this level who will welcome you. Now you will commence an entirely different life from this point. There has not been much communication from spirit from the Mental Levels as they are beyond what we could fully understand at this time. I feel they try to impress us with thoughts when needing guidance rather than trying to communicate through a medium as they have to go through the process of coming down through the levels to reach our slower and denser vibration.

I do not blame them not really wanting to do this. It is a bit like us living in a natural, beautiful paradise and going to a barren lifeless place; I know which one I would choose. This is not to say there are those whose love for humankind would not go to this barren place if they felt they could be of service to help plant a few seeds, to cultivate the land to teach those who wish to learn.

Mental World

This is like promotion to the upper floors/levels.

As I have already said the time comes when we have the transition from the Astral to the Mental Level. Leaving our Astral vehicle behind is like peeling an onion, the first layer is the Physical Body the second the Astral Body, the third the Mental, Emotional Body and finally to the Core, the Causal Body. The Mental Body is made of even a finer substance than the Astral Body. It is more of a thought form of ourselves, this is again beyond our comprehension to try and visualise this.

As with the passing from the earth, we do not always realise that we have passed onto the Mental Level. The peace and tranquillity you feel is indescribable. When you are in the Mental Worlds it is as if you are linking into a radio but you are the radio. You are able to transmit your thoughts and receive other's thoughts. You are able to link to like-minded people and are able to have interesting and lively conversation with people who wish to join in with similar knowledge and interests. Depending on how evolved you are decides how long you stay on this level. For those who have no interest in intellectual ideas at this time would find this level boring and would only stay on these levels for a short time. For those who desire for more knowledge stay for however long they wish, moving up the seven levels, maybe taking their new-found knowledge into future lives. There are seven levels of consciousness, just as there are in the Astral Level. Normally you will go to the Sphere that suits you. You are able to move up or down but invariably you stay on the same level until it is time to drop the Mental Body when you go onto the Causal Level.

Causal Level

The board room.

The third transition is the same as the previous two. You just fall asleep and wake up on this level. This is your ego, your true self. On this level all your memories of previous lives remain. Each incarnation adds more experience to the

Causal Body. This fountain of knowledge can be accessed if the person is Spiritually evolved enough while he is on earth. This can enable us to avoid having to repeat certain things in each life, as normally with each new life we have no memory of past experiences. The more spiritually evolved the person, the more advantages you may have over less evolved souls. This is where we can be of great use and service to others in guidance and in love. At this level all is at one, the past, present and future. I will give you an example. There is a mountain. If you stand at the bottom of this mountain and start to climb up it, you will only see what is just around the bend, beyond that you cannot see (the future). When the person is at the top of the mountain he sees the whole, past, present and future. He sees the landscape in the now whereas the person climbing the mountain is the past and present. This is the difference between an evolved soul and an un-evolved soul. But we are all striving for the same goal and we will all reach it: how and when is not important.

The Causal Level is the most wonderful level of all but the time comes when we have to move on with accordance of natural law. This desire will happen naturally; we will want to progress, experience and further our knowledge, which we know has to include more earthly lives. This will have to continue until we reach the time when it will be unnecessary to have to be reborn to earth. We can then move onto more spiritual activities on higher spheres. Some still out of love for mankind will still wish to serve earth and stay in touch with our vibration to help our evolution. I suspect that if it weren't for these beautiful souls we would become quite stagnant and be very slow with our progression.

Communication, as we go higher would be beyond our human understanding. I am sure there are some who could possibly tap into these levels. So I will leave this to others to write on this subject if they have this awareness.

When it is time to reincarnate back to earth you have to re-clothe yourselves, starting with a Mental Body, which encompasses your intellect. This is why some people seem more intellectual than others do, their knowledge they have attained is that much more evolved. This is not to say they are more worthy, if anything they have more responsibility to others to help them towards their goals. Next is the Astral Body, emotional progress is encompassed to this body, as are new talents you may have learnt whilst on the Astral Planes. This is why some people seem so natural at certain gifts. Next is the Physical Body. The necessary channel for birth. You and higher ones as I have suggested have decided this and on which country you will be born into. Every country has its own special attributes to offer which ordains the problems which each soul will have to deal with. These may be problems with health, shortage of money, food, prejudices against you, just to name a few, which may have to be overcome. The only certainty is that we are never left to choose or face challenges which are greater than our strength to combat them. If you look back in history you will see how many people have overcome what would seem immovable obstacles and blocks in their paths. How much they have achieved in the end has seemed quite an amazing feat.

This is a lesson for us all, there is nothing we cannot overcome if we have the right attitude and use the full energy of love.

Peace and Love

Ankh - Regeneration of Life Through Water

This is an Egyptian symbols that represents eternal life. It also means the regeneration of life through water. The loop at the top of this sign signifies holy water circulating continuously. It is also known as the key of the Nile or a cross with a handle, the breath of life.

Please visit my website:-
www.f-a-c-e-life.com
www.spiritualtherapies.co.uk
or email me at **suejhewitt@gmail.com**
if you have any questions or wish to enquire about my circles and my workshops.

Printed in Great Britain
by Amazon